Boxer's SHORTS

(More Than Just A Brief)
Attempt At Humor

Boxer's Shorts

(More Than Just A Brief)
Attempt At Humor

Punchline Press, Inc
Wilmette, Illinois

CREATED BY ROBERT BOXER M.D.
ILLUSTRATED BY DARNELL TOWNS

Manuscript Editor
Carole Isaacs

Book and Cover Design
David Corona Design/ Carlisle Communications, Ltd.

Typesetting and Production Services
Carlisle Communications, Ltd.

Cover Illustration
Darnell Towns

Back Cover Photograph
Frank McMahon

Published by Punchline Press, Inc.
P.O. Box 6058, Wilmette, IL 60091

Printed in the United States of America

First Edition, October, 1988

Library of Congress catalog no.: 88–90962
ISBN: 0–9620687–0–5

Contents

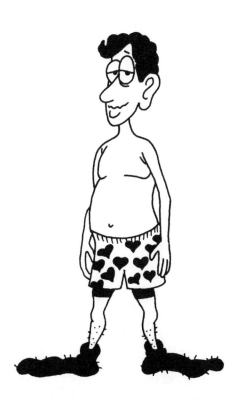

Dedications

To my wife, Marsha, and my sons, Stephen and Richard, for their love, and for their reluctant, but nevertheless very real, support in making this book a reality.

To my late beloved parents, Minnie and Isadore Boxer, whose sense of humor and love and guidance contributed in a very basic and immeasurable way to make this book possible.

To Esther Berg, of Prairie Village, Kansas, a very dear and special friend.

To punsters everywhere who have taken sadistic delight in making people just a little bit uncomfortable.

Illustrator's Dedication

To my family, especially my parents, Eddie and Cleola Towns, and my grandmother, Rena Martin, and my brother, John, for without watching him draw all these years, I would be drawing stick figures.

Foreword

Even though all children are embarrassed by their parents at times in their lives, I have endured much more than my fair share. Throughout my life (all twenty-one years of it), my Dad has never failed to embarrass me and my family. Whether it be in the company of our friends, relatives, or worse yet, total strangers, he has always managed to "pun", resulting in the groans and forced smiles of all those present. You see, punning is my Dad's pride and joy. He has been doing it all of his life, but rather than improving, he just keeps getting worse.

For a while, we wondered if he was going through a mid-life crisis, and then this crazy idea for a book came along, and that clinched it. Believe it or not, the puns contained herein represent only a small portion of my Dad's repertoire, which at times seem to number in the millions. To some people, these are the best of a bad lot, but to my Dad, they are the realization of the dream of a lifetime. So just remember as you read this book, that it could have been worse. And Dad, you remember: this is it!, this is your dream come true. I know you will make the most of it, because you never do things "just for the halibut".

Stephen A. Boxer.

Preface

It was only recently when I sat down to write this preface, just days before it was due at the printer, that I realized for the first time that it may actually have been my early life experiences with an unusual name which were responsible for a keener-than-usual passion for puns. Perhaps the world might have been spared, had my name been Smith.

Even though the pun is regarded by some to be the lowest form of humor, I've always considered it an enjoyable challenge. Although I was punning substantially earlier, I really became a "serious punner" during my days as a medical student at Northwestern University.

Although many people have winced and almost cried, I eventually found that I was making some people laugh, including patients, friends, and fellow physicians, consistently enough that I decided I had better start recording some of my ideas. But instead of merely recording the text, I felt that I could enhance the humor by illustrating the pun.

It seems that there is a current proliferation of puns in the newspapers, radio, T.V., and in advertising media in general. This suggests that an appreciation of puns is more widespread than most people would like to admit.

We are all aware that a sense-of-humor is meaningful in all areas of life. We are now beginning to recognize that humor has particular therapeutic value in the field of medicine. I think that the ability of a physician to appropriately "inject" humor into the care of patients in a tasteful and considerate manner is clearly an asset.

I feel very fortunate in having found Darnell Towns, a talented young animator, filmmaker, and illustrator, who has cleverly and creatively drawn my thoughts. I hope that those who read this book will enjoy the blending of humor and art.

"How long have you considered
yourself a sex symbol?"

1

"No, those aren't the tablets I told you to take."

"I'll have the Peking Duck".

"I told you not to play with that outlet; now you're really grounded!"

"......striking out with two out in the bottom of the ninth and the bases loaded. Now do you understand what a Cardinal sin is?"

"I'm really angry at that artist, he chiseled me out of a great deal of money."

6

"We finally found the rattle in your car".

"I see Coach Smith has put in all of his subs".

"Tonto, have you figured out how to save a buck yet?"

"Is this what the Professor meant by
'Statutory rape'?"

"You must be looking for the Bridle path."

"You can bet that with men on base, when Abraham comes up to bat... he'll sacrifice".

"I try to be a 'roll model' for my kids."

"I'm writing this book on puns called 'Annie get your pun' and I'm in a hurry! Do you have any Quick draw artists?"

16

"We're going to have to take down the outside antenna, we're getting too many humans on the screen".

"With your diplomatic immunity,
I'm surprised you caught it."

"So that's how Jim picks up his spares".

"I understand you're trying to minimize
your 'out-of-pocket' expenses."

Designer Genes

TOUCHE!

TOUPÉE!

created by Robert Boxer M.D.
ILLUSTRATED BY DARNELL TOWNS

© Robert Boxer 1986

"Well Doctor, you did ask me to design a low key office for you".

Baseball, a game of inches.

"Well, you did ask Jill to bring home
some Liquid Plumber, didn't you?"

"I'm sorry. We can't today. We're really swamped".

"Now you're really splitting Hairs!"

"You're being charged with Grand Theft!"

"That's how they're taught to file suits".

"Darnell, please draw these pornographic cartoons and dedicate them to sin".

"Great! I have always wanted to be a Sin-dedicated cartoonist."

"It's like I said, Incredible reception, don't you agree?"

"I just can't understand why you would need a studfinder."

"No Dear, I'm not on my mobile phone, but I am stuck in the middle of a bridge."

33

"Our boss is an expert on Employee Retention."

"Better not even think twice about her....she's definitely a Gold digger."

"Now the relative humidity is 100%."

"How's that for a perfect textbook landing?"

"Be careful, Honey....it's a jungle out there".

"A Classic Case of Mercury Poisoning."

"Doc, if it's true that your body is your temple, then I want to change religions."

"Well yes, I did ask for a micro-wave for the office".

"They really brought him up from the minors".

"That's great, the Archdiocese has just ordered a whole fleet of Conversion Vans".

43

"If he doesn't keep up his payments, his car is <u>really</u> going to be repossessed."

44

"I'd like ta 'elp yew lose a hundred pounds".

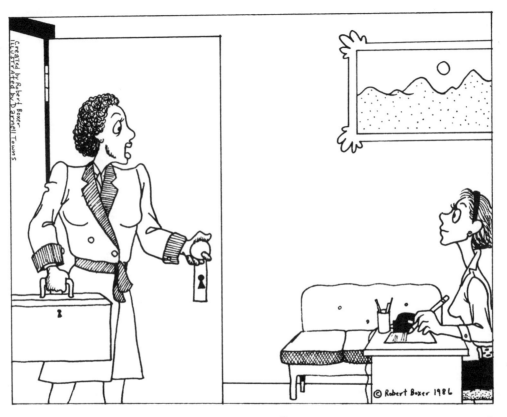

"I'm expecting return calls from both my gynecologist and my interior decorator. Be sure you know who's calling if the message is `It's curtains'."

47

49

"I picked this up atta flea market".

"IF I could just get off the Dam phone".

53

A Cardiac Arrest

"I can see that the company has adopted a two-teared payscale."

"I should've known when that Guy walked
in and told me he was an Options Trader."

"You won't believe how muggy it is outside".

"This is the first true wildcat strike I've ever seen."

"Yeah doc, the pressure is mounting".

A FREUDIAN SLIP

"I'm going to put an end to this strike."   "Ok Darnell, Draw!"

"Careful Len, don't make a spectacle of yourself."

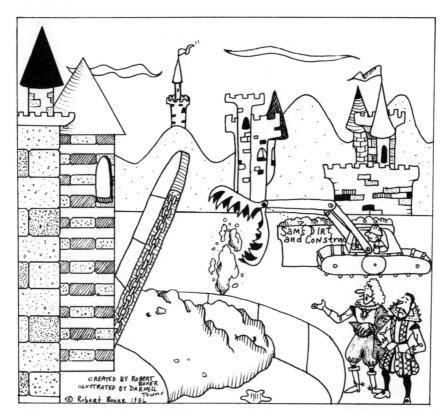

"I guess he's being de-moated."

"You should consider working in a photography studio; you appear to be so negative."

"I sure hope she's not out of Heet yet."

"You're either blind or generous to a fault".

WZBN-NEWS

"There was flooding in Wisconsin today and reporter Jim Novak went to Oshkosh to get an overall view."

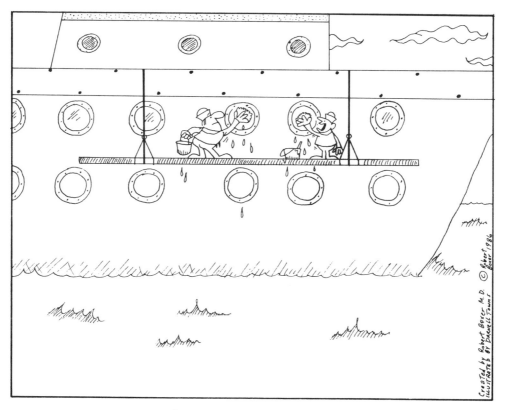

"The nice thing about this job is that we get porthole to porthole pay."

"Maybe you're allergic to Cello mold".

Sunday Flee Market

"I'm not really interested in these two suitors, but tell me how much is that Overnight bag?"

"Wow! These prices are Astronomical!"

"I'm speaking to Dr. Fred Bury from the Board of Health and he informs me that if the strike isn't settled soon, there may be grave consequences".

"Somebody said that there was an opening at first base".

"Better go for change, I can see they all have big bills".

"Bob, your humor is so dry, it's crackin' up the furniture".

"30 degrees southeast, 45 knot speed.... I sure hope they don't find out I'm a Stool pigeon."

"The Medical director is upset because this New doctor has diagnosed everyone as having a Miner lung problem."

"Valerie always tries to eat a
well-balanced breakfast."

"The Administration is really determined to stop leaks from the White House".

"I've been assigned the task of investigating Bouncing Czechs."

"I didn't mean to worry you about your blood pressure, it was just an off-the-cuff remark."

"Well... You did tell me to call a Roofer."

"I was told not to audition unless I had several films under my belt."

"April, did you order that just for the Halibut?"

"Well Christine, you wanted to be an Anchorwoman—did'nt you?"

"Watch this guy, he usually crashes on the last lap".

"I just hate to see my prophets going down the drain".

"He's so good looking. I felt like
I was putty in his hands".

"Darnell, Tommy the turtle is too bashful".

"That's why I'm trying to draw him out of his shell".

"You two will have to use the double doors".

BABY BOOM

"Well, you can't say we weren't warned".

"The coach said, 'Now go out there and try to draw a FouL'".

"Can't a girl just try to turn a **Prophet?!**"

"Now I'll have to find another vehicle for my humor."

"Now that's what I call a real gallop pole".

"Aaron! Stop that Idol gossip!"

"I think this Organ transplantation program is a wonderful idea".

TRULY A CINDERELLA TEAM

"I just can't go through one more revolution."

"This is not at all what I had in mind for Elizabeth".

"Now that's what I call a real Scholarship".

"It looks like this course is going to turn out to be a 'Test of Wills'."

"I bet he doesn't even Know I'm Dead."

114

"This group doesn't intimidate me, Sergeant,
I'm used to working with Rough Drafts."

"This is my only **Asset**."

"They have decided to sever their Family Ties".

117

"I brought this for those interested in more definition."

"This computer makes Spelling easy, I just move the Cursor from name to name."

Created by Robert Boxer M.D.
Illustrated by Darnell Towns

"The Pitching coach is especially interested in Larkin with his unusual wind-up".

Acknowledgements
(The Guilty Parties)

Many, many must share the blame for this book because of their support and encouragement, intentional or unintentional. The following are the guilty parties: My wife Marsha, who could have and should have stopped me, if necessary even threatening to leave me, instead of enduring my puns in public, over many years; my eldest son Stephen, who reviewed puns and otherwise helped, but at least had enough sense to accuse me of wasting considerable money in this pursuit. The many promises Stephen extracted from me guaranteeing that I would not pun in front of his friends did not sufficiently deter me; my other son Richard, who not only reviewed potential puns, but also contributed many ideas to this book. In Rick's defense, however, he did label most of my puns "absolutely not funny", "forget it", "no Dad", "no way", "work on it", and other derisions; my mother-in-law, Rose Levin, of Cincinnati, for her interest; Elliott and Shelly Abramson for consistently providing valued encouragement (perhaps more than any others, they must shoulder the burden for the existence of this book); Bill and Zehava Frankel for helping in so many ways. Bill is a copyright attorney whose advice has been invaluable; Joe Sugarman for his ideas and encouragement. Joe, a successful entrepreneur, author, and speaker, can particularly be blamed for fostering the illusion that I could be successful at being funny; my office nurses, both present and past, Susan Heidenreich, Mary Buckley, Diane Plennert, Shari Charnogorsky, Grace Holt, and Judi Erickson, for tolerating and even laughing at my puns; Judi's husband, Mark for also suggesting the title, "Boxer's Shorts"; Susan especially for having helped make the office run efficiently during the time the book was created, freeing up a little time

and peace of mind for me to work on this book; my medical and lunch colleagues at Rush North Shore Medical Center for occasionally laughing, thus promoting and encouraging my relentless punning, particularly Doctors Leonard Berlin, Michael Nagel, Josh Epstein, Larry Maillis, David Appert, Howard Woolf, Clair Malcolm Rice, Richard Geline, Wayne Wirtz, Eugene Goldman, Jack Mozdzen, Mike Capek, Shelly Miller, Narciso Lobo, Gary Novetsky, Elliott Goldin, Bob Eng, Morton Doblin, Bernard Hankin, David Lee, Arnie Swerdlow, Bob Gara, Herb Lipschultz, Michael Lewis, Harold Laker, Arkady Rapoport, Sushil Sharma, Abe Chervony, and Leigh Rosenblum; Doctor Thomas Affeldt, for his persistent interest and encouragement.

Other people who must share the blame for this book include the following: Mary Ann Bodine and Barbara Haefke for typing thousands of puns, most of which were not good enough to be in this book. They both missed a legitimate opportunity to summon help; Georgia Photopulos, a remarkable writer, author, and friend, for her inspiration and support; Jody Yeh, for her encouragement and for giving me the idea for the cartoon on page 69; Carole Isaacs, a clever and creative copy editor who provided valuable editorial assistance as well as encouragement; Jim Sanders, of Carlisle Communications who assisted editorially, and appreciated the humor; Harvey Gordon, for writing a number of successful and very funny pun cartoon books that helped to inspire this book; "The International Save the Pun Foundation" and its hard working and uniquely creative Chairman, John S. Crosbie, for the

foundation's monthly newsletters, and Joyce Heitler, the innovative Chicago Chapter Organizer, for the annual dinners, both of which serve to encourage punsters like me to continue; Darnell Towns, the illustrator, for depicting my creations with such originality and humor that I was continuously spurred on; Janet, Steve, and Brian Altman, Judy Bartuch, Amanda Bernstein, Carolyn and Tom Stone, Christine Moriarity, Ed Hult, LeRoy Kwiatt, Penni Berman, Ronald Siegel, Harold Bosmann, Sandie Demos, Barbara Kravets, Eulalia Adam, Judy West, Nan Bloom, Anshel Gostomelsky, Carol Hopwood, Donna Murphy, Gwen Ott, Jack Isaacs, Nate Wagner, Roberta Berkowitz, Andrew Fisher, Evelyn Winfield, Pat Brown, and Meg Barth, all friends, for their interest.

Finally, George Pattison, editor of "The Main Event, Monthly Sports Journal for Physicians" deserves the ultimate blame for regularly publishing a number of my pun cartoons incorporating medicine and sports. Had I ever thought of quitting, seeing my creations in print dispelled any such inclination.

The only person who truly deserves credit for sincerely trying to dissuade me is my very dear Aunt Mary Nieman from Cincinnati. Aunt Mary spent endless hours and hours reviewing hundreds of cartoons and concluded that only two were even remotely funny. The world owes her for at least trying, although unsuccessfully, to discourage me.

Disclaimer

To the best of my knowledge, all of the ideas for the cartoons in this book are original. At the time of their conception, I was unaware of any previous similar ideas. Obviously, no one can be totally aware of all prior or present ideas in existence, and because of that, and in spite of my claim of originality, I beg forgiveness from those who are offended by the knowledge that they have been much cleverer and at an earlier date than I, and I accept the probability of that reality.

About the Author

Dr. Robert W. Boxer is a practicing allergist, with offices in the Professional Building of the Old Orchard Center in Skokie, Illinois, a suburb of Chicago. Bob has created thousands of pun cartoons and in the last several years a number of these have been published. Dr. Boxer graduated from Southwest High School in Kansas City, Missouri, and earned his pre-medical degree at the University of Denver. He obtained his Medical Degree from Northwestern University Medical School, served his internship and residency at Cook County Hospital in Chicago, and trained in allergy at the University of Illinois College of Medicine in Chicago. He is on the medical staffs of Lutheran General Hospital in Park Ridge, Illinois, and Rush North Shore Medical Center in Skokie, Illinois. Dr. Boxer is a Clinical Associate in medicine at the University of Illinois College of Medicine in Chicago. He is a fellow of the American Academy of Allergy and Immunology, the American College of Allergy and Immunology, the American Association of Board Certified Allergists, the Illinois Society of Allergy and Immunology, and the American Academy of Environmental Medicine. He is a member of the American Medical Association and the Illinois State and Chicago Medical Societies. Dr. Boxer is on the Professional Advisory Board of the "Nutrition for Optimal Health Association ", and is a member of Alpha Omega Alpha, Honor Medical Society. He is, of course, also a member of "The International Save the Pun Foundation".

Bob's pun cartoons, illustrated by Darnell Towns, appear regularly in "The Main Event, Monthly Sports Journal for Physicians".

About the Illustrator

Darnell Towns graduated from The School of the Art Institute of Chicago, with a B.F.A. in Filmmaking and Animation. Born and raised on Chicago's South side, Darnell began drawing at an early age. He attended Wendell Phillip's High School, where he excelled in his art classes.

Currently, Mr. Towns is freelancing as an animator and a caricaturist, and is teaching cartooning at Hyde Park Art Center.

When Darnell first responded to Bob's inquiry through The School of the Art Institute of Chicago, he was curious, since he could not imagine a physician with a sense of humor. While most people know better, in this instance Darnell's skepticism may have been well founded.

List of Cartoons

1. Sex Symbol
2. Tablets to Take
3. Peking Duck
4. You're Really Grounded
5. Cardinal Sin
6. Chiseled Out of Money
7. Fly Fishing
8. Rattle In Car
9. Swat Team
10. Put In All Subs
11. Loan Arranger
12. Statutory Rape
13. Bridle Path
14. Abraham Sacrifices
15. Roll Model
16. Quick Draw Artist
17. Humans On The Screen
18. Diplomatic Immunity
19. Pick Up Spares
20. Out-Of-Pocket Expenses
21. Designer Genes
22. "Touche! Toupee!"
23. Low Key Office
24. Game Of Inches
25. Liquid Plumber
26. Really Swamped
27. Splitting Hairs
28. Grand Theft
29. File Suits
30. Sin-Dedicated Cartoonist
31. Incredible Reception
32. Stud Finder
33. Middle Of A Bridge
34. Employee Retention
35. Gold Digger
36. Relative Humidity
37. Text Book Landing
38. Jungle Out There
39. Mercury Poisoning
40. Change Religions
41. Microwave For Office
42. Up From The Minors
43. Conversion Vans
44. Really Repossessed
45. Lose 100 Pounds
46. "How Not To Split Up"
47. It's Curtains
48. Inflated Ego
49. Just My Coffin
50. Atta Flea Market
51. Dam Phone
52. Stoned Crab
53. No Spare Time
54. A Cardiac Arrest

55. Two-Teared Pay Scale
56. Options Trader
57. Muggy Outside
58. True Wild Cat Strike
59. Pressure Is Mounting
60. A Freudian Slip
61. "OK Darnell, Draw"
62. Spectacle Of Yourself
63. Being De-Moated
64. Appear Negative
65. Out Of Heet Yet
66. Generous To A Fault
67. An Overall View
68. Porthole Pay
69. Cello Mold
70. Sunday Flee Market
71. Tent Tire Sale
72. Overnight Bag
73. Poached Fish
74. Astronomical Prices
75. Other Line
76. Grave Consequences
77. First Base
78. Take A Hike
79. Big Bills
80. Crackin' Up Furniture
81. Stool Pigeon

82. Miner Lung Problem
83. Balanced Breakfast
84. White House Leaks
85. Bouncing Czechs
86. Off-The-Cuff Remark
87. Homebound Listeners
88. Call A Roofer
89. Films Under Belt
90. Date Of First Pun
91. Anchorwoman
92. Last Lap Crash
93. No Free Launch
94. Prophets Down Drain
95. Putty In His Hands
96. Mussel-Bound
97. Draw Out Of His Shell
98. Double Doors
99. Tide Coming In
100. Baby Boom
101. Catch Basin
102. Draw A Foul
103. Turn A Prophet
104. Vehicle For Humor
105. Real Gallop Pole
106. Idol Gossip
107. Organ Transplantation
108. Cinderella Team

Book Order Form

**Attention:
Schools and Businesses**

Punchline Press™ books are available at quantity discounts with bulk purchase for educational, business, or sales promotional use. For information, please write to Special Sales Dept., Punchline Press, Inc., Box 6058, Wilmette, IL 60091.

BOXER'S SHORTS (More Than Just A Brief Attempt At Humor)
This book is available at fine book stores, or by sending $7.95, plus $1.00 to cover postage and handling, to the following address: Punchline Press, Inc., P.O. Box 6058, Wilmette, Illinois, 60091.

Please send me _____ books at
$7.95* each $ _____

Illinois residents add 7% sales tax $ _____

Add $1.00 for shipping and handling $ **1.00**_____

                                            Total $ _____

Check or money order made payable to Punchline Press, Inc.

Name _____

Address _____

City _____

State _____

Country _____

Zip Code _____

*(Prices subject to change without notice)
Order subject to availability.
Please allow four to six weeks for delivery.
All amounts are in U.S. Dollars.